Praying it Forward

loving your grandchildren through prayer!

by Caryn Southerland and friends

Dedication: To Fern Nichols, founder

and faithful leader of Moms In Prayer International. Fern has called us to become prayer-iors FOR our children/their schools and teachers WITH God. MIPI is now 30 years stronger and we are now grandmothers, even more dedicated to praying for our families. This privilege and practice of prayer is still teaching us WHO our God is and the joy of being His. May our book, <u>Praying It Forward</u>,- <u>loving our grandchildren through prayer</u> represent a boomerang blessing to both her and our God.

These prayers are especially for my grandchild:

_____

Prayed in love, confidence, & joy from:

_____

Introduction

Greetings, blessings and welcome to our prayer time! Hold on, sister *grand,* we have so much to experience as we jump in the Word with God and approach Him on behalf of our priceless treasures! I have a feeling that by book's end, you will have discovered a new level and a deeper definition of prayer that is wonderfully indescribable; a definition that springboards you into using scripture as the inspiration of a constant conversation with God (perhaps a more appropriate description of prayer!)

God IS calling you and me to Himself. His Word is evident and repetitious with invitation to enter into relationship with Him, which translates into perpetual conversation. What better subject to talk about than our grandchildren? Who better to talk to than the One who generously gifted us with them?

I pray you find "bonus beyond" in the time you spend praying for them. I pray you find a Friend like none other; so soul satisfying. (This prayer booklet can be more than just about grandchildren!) The more I draw near to Him the more I confidently conclude that He longs to hear our voices (a sound like none other to Him); it is His greatest pleasure, His desire, and His hope and enjoyment in partnership with us. Don't we long to hear our grandchildren's voices and see their arms extended to us? Don't we delight in relationship with our grandchildren?

I hope you can relate when I say that my grandchildren are easy to love and I do crazy things when I have them. I surprise myself! Released and free to be foolishly in love, embarrassingly so! May I say to you – your inner core – that God so wants you to know He feels that way about you! Yes, this book is more than just about your grandchildren; it can be about your relationship with the One who is crazy about you and so willing to prove it to you. Chance it! As you participate, I encourage you to allow those thoughts or even questions to surface. Avail yourself to be loved along with your grandchildren. A grand connection – a powerful surge going in two directions that can only make us outrageously grander!

One last point: we are made in His image: emotional, mental, physical, and spiritual. This is the grand connection and the opportunity to capitalize on it. To relate to Him in this way taps into the resource of power as join Him in through our prayers. Meeting Him here positively changes our family, God's Kingdom, and us: to love like He loves, speak like He speaks, pray like He prays. Now, that is an irresistible invitation!

So thrilled you are joining me and the many other moms of grandeur status to release agreement (prayer) WITH God FOR our grandchildren. Each introduces herself and her unique "grand name" in the prayer times ahead. Enjoy your time with the One who can't wait to meet you in these pages and share secrets and strategies that magnetize your heart to His. Grand exploits await you! (I hear that "Yes" coming forth from you and I "Amen" you heartily.)

Just a little explanation and a little instruction...

This could be a beginning in many ways for you. If you have never studied the Word of God the treat of your life is yet ahead. This is meant to be easy, attractive, and very addictive! I want to explain a little about the format, the reason behind it, and how to use it with grand hopes that your experience in partnership with the Lord will be extravagant.

I encourage you to set aside about an hour for each prayer time. (Having the same time of the day - or if you are planning once a week- always helps me to stay consistent.)

Invite another "grand" friend (s) to join you. Grab your bibles, a pen, and perhaps a tissue! Just start at the top and continue through the page. The four steps of prayer should guide you. Simple as that!

Let's go, then – we shall start using a format called the Four Steps of Prayer:

Praise, Confession, Thanksgiving, and Petition. You remember - the way Jesus answered when asked by the disciples how to pray! Each page will be laid out in this way with a booster start: a name of God or a name of Jesus as a subject for

Praise. Scriptures will reference how God describes Himself. Look them up and share your personal thoughts, comments, or revelations on and the blank lines. Letting God spoon feed us insight about Himself will thrill our soul and start our prayer time with both confidence and humility – the perfect balance and blessing for petitioning Him later for our grandchildren. Let your mouth follow with a voiced awe of WHO He IS. As you speak and acknowledge who God is, as He says He is, it is like throwing open the door, laying down the mat and saying yes to the most worthy and life changing of endeavors. The God of Glory will come in and bring His Kingdom with Him. (Praising Him; it is really harder to stop than it is to start!)   Time: 10 - 12 minutes

Confession follows the praise time and it is suggested to be a 180 degrees turn around. By that I mean that your focus changes from God to YOU and your tongue becomes silent. Just you and the One, you have now invited with your praises, sit together reviewing and reversing those things that have separated you both. His presence requires a clean seat! This time of confession is perhaps the most powerful because of the precious peace it affords.

A time to just be quiet before Him by yourself or even in the midst of others – letting the Word, His Word, wash over you and wash away the guilt, shame, wrong thinking and heaviness of them all. This silent moment is essential – because His magnificent voice speaks in caressing tones of forgiveness, cleansing, and restoration. New energy returns to your spirit and body as real as if you had a physical shower with water and soap making you presentable to not just Him, but to yourself! You are huggable and want to be hugged! Your God is first in line! Time: 2-3 minutes

Thanksgiving: is a natural after-flow of confession. Your tongue is now released to share the bounty of His giving   the many things God has done! He provided, orchestrated, opened and shut doors. He planned rewards that thrill us and leave us shaking our heads with wonder and grateful disbelief of how timely, personal, and generous He is. Sharing this in prayer with others is a certain way of heightening the atmosphere and allowing the contagious spirit of appreciation stir hearts in preparation for the next step! Time: 10 –12 minutes.

Petition. All channels are clear now to ask of God – the place we usually start our prayers. Yet, after our time of positioning Him as the subject of our praises and ourselves to be cleansed, forgiven, and restored; then a time of grateful reflection (thanksgiving) , our prayers take on an added fervency and confidence that just doesn't happen otherwise! We will use the same Word of God that was our focus to praise Him only now, to pray for our grandchildren. We will speak it back to Him in the form of a petition that has more of the sound of a most respectful declaration rather than a pleading. We will place our grandchildren's name in the scriptures and ask in a spirit of believing. This may be awkward at first, but it will not take long!   Isaiah 55:11 proclaims that His Word never returns void, likening it to raindrops that water the earth to bring forth life. A beautiful picture of each drop like each prayer sustaining and refreshing the little life we have been given.

Following the scripture petition, you will have lots of space to record your specific prayers for your grandchild. This section will make this journal truly personal as well as a possible future gift for your grandchild. You may want to use this either as a journal for yester-year reflection or you may want to write directly to them little notes or letters of affection. Wouldn't you (and I) love to have the captured prayers and thoughts of our grandmothers!

If you are praying with another grandmom, you may want to have a notebook handy to jot a reminder of their specific prayers, so that you can join them in their requests.. This also allows you to participate with others and yet keep your book personal for your grandchild.

I suggest praying for one grandchild at a time - just as if you placed them individually the middle of your circle. As you take turns reading the scripture, put their names in the blanks provided. Allow the grandmother of that child to next pray her specific prayers over her grandchild. Others follow with agreement prayers or added petitions, as they feel led. Each grandmother takes a turn until each child has been saturated with prayer.   Time: 20 – 25 minutes

Names
Of
God

Yahweh

El Emmunah

El Ohim

El Elyon

Jehovah Jireh

Jehovah Roi

Jehovah Rapha

Jehovah Shalom

Jehovah Tsidkenu

Jehovah Shammah

Jehovah Nissi

Jehovah Rophe

Yahweh...I Am

"It's Me," says the Lord who calls Himself YAHWEH. If God has a first name, a familiar one, to make Himself inviting, it would be YAHWEH! He IS (as we are in our grandmother glory) more interested in being "known" than showing off! Just as we (with tender excitement) would announce our identity to our grandchild on the phone, God is saying that His name, most intimately familiar is YAHWEH! I feel Him tenderly grab our faces and stare into our eyes repeating, "It's Me, Yahweh," until we receive totally that wonderful, power packed reality.

Hello, I cherish being the grandmother of two girls who know me as MeMe! I love calling them and saying it's me – and they know who it is their MeMe ! (also known as Caryn Southerland.) I invite you into the depths of God's "favorite way to be known" name: YAHWEH (my personal, unsubstantiated opinion!)

Praise: (10-15 min.) YAHWEH

Definition: "I AM" Hebrew = ha yah which is a form of "to be" and only used when referring to God. This Hebrew word also means "was", "is", and "will be", as in forever.

Here are scriptures where Yahweh is used rather than the generic God we read in our versions; use them for your time of praise.

Psalm 27: 1-4; Exodus 3: 13-15, 6: 2-3; Genesis 2: 4-7;

Isaiah 61: 10-11

Personal thoughts:

_____

_____

_____

_____

Confession: (2-3 silent min.)

   Please just bow your head and speak silently with Yahweh in a spirit of agreement regarding the actions, thoughts, events that have separated you from Him. Let Him direct you back to Himself by His promise to forgive, cleanse, and restore.

Hosea 14:1,2 Return oh, grandmother, to Yahweh, your God. Your sins have been your downfall! Take words with you and return to Yahweh. Say to Him, "forgive all my sins and receive me graciously that I may offer the fruit of my lips."

Hosea 14:5-7 "I shall cure, I shall love you with all my heart, I shall restore, " says Yahweh.

Thanksgiving: (10-15 min.)

Psalm 50:23 She (grandmothers) who sacrifice thank offerings honors Me and prepares the way so that I may show her the salvation of Yahweh.

Pour out your thanks to Him for all the ways, things, and blessings He has provided this week for your grandchildren. Share them out loud with those around you so that He may be honored and they, too, may be encouraged.

_____

_____

_____

_____

Petition: (20 – 25 min.)

Psalm 116: 12-13. How can I repay the Lord for all His acts of kindness to me? I will celebrate my deliverance and call on the name (Yahweh) of the Lord.

This is our time of placing our grandchildren in the presence of Yahweh, calling on Him. We partner with Him by declaring/praying His Word and we then add specifics in our own language. Friends or family who are praying with you may want to agree with your prayers and add something they may feel prompted to ask. If there are two or more, please take turns praying for each other's grandchildren, reading the Word over them and then adding your personal requests. This is not a time to hurry – rather linger with the Lord and each other to saturate your children with prayer.

Scripture (taken from our praise time) Psalm 27: 1-4

Yahweh is _____'s light and his/her salvation, whom shall _____ fear?

Yahweh is the stronghold of _____'s life, of whom shall

_____ be afraid?

When evil men advance against _____
to devour his/her flesh, when
_____ enemies and his/her foes
attack _____.

Though an army besiege
_____, he/she will not
fear, though war break out against
_____, even then will he/she be
confident.

One thing _____ will ask of

Yahweh, this is what _____

seeks: that he/she will dwell in the house of Yahweh

all the days of his/her life to gaze upon the beauty of

Yahweh and seek Him in His temple.

My special and specific requests:

_____

_____

_____

_____

My thoughts and loving declarations:

_____

_____

_____

_____

Jehovah Tsidkenu...
Righteousness

When my first grandchild was born, my husband soon told our friends, "Jan has gone bonkers!" I have to admit he was right. I had no idea the joy and delight this little one would bring. Not only are grandchildren a gift from God in *our* lives, He has given *us* the wonderful privilege, as grandmothers, of pouring into *their* lives the life and truth of God through our words, actions and prayers. That's why I chose the name, Granna, for my grandchildren to call me. It is a combination of Gran and Anna; the one who lived in the temple as an intercessor. I love my new role!

As we look at God's Name, Jehovah Tsidkenu—the Lord our Righteousness, how thankful I am that we no longer have to adhere to the stringent demands of the law of Old Testament grandmothers. Can you imagine taking your grandchildren with you to present your animal sacrifices to the priests for the covering of your sins? What a gruesome, but necessary, requirement they had to follow, for 'without the shedding of blood there is no remission of sin'. Thanks be to God He made a better way for us through the sacrifice of His Son, Jesus Christ. God knew all along that there was no way we could be righteous on our own. The law only exposed this truth to us. We needed a Righteous One to be righteousness for us. Now, because of what Christ has done, we stand holy and blameless in the sight of God. Jesus very own righteousness has been imputed to us. The blood of Jesus cleanses us from ALL unrighteousness.

Praise: (10-15 min.)

Definition: **Jehovah Tsidkenu:** to make right, to clear or cleanse, to justify

Scriptures: Jeremiah 23:5-6, Romans. 1:17, 5:17, 10:3-4, I Corinthians 1:30, II Corinthian s 5:21

What a blessing to be able to share this Good News with our grandchildren. They now have One who will live in them, both to be their righteousness *and* give them power to live good and holy lives. The Accuser no longer can heap guilt and condemnation on them (or us). I love what Derek Prince says, '*Guilt is the key to our defeat and righteousness is the key to our victory!*'

As we receive God's abundant provision of grace and believe the truth that the Lord Himself is our Righteousness, He brings abundant life for both our grandchildren and us! Let's praise!

Personal thoughts:

_____

_____

_____

_____

Confession: (2-3 silent min.)

As grandmothers and human beings, we are well aware that we fall short of God's glorious ideal for us, we sin. I John 2:1-2 states that 'if anybody does sin, we have one who speaks to the Father in our defense—Jesus Christ, the Righteous One. He is the atoning sacrifice for our sins and not only for ours but also for the sins of the whole world. Confession is not a time to wallow in despair over our failures, it is a time to receive God's abundant provision of grace and gift of righteousness and reign in life through Jesus Christ our Lord.

Romans 5:17

Thanksgiving: (10-15 min.)

God has blessed us with incalculable gifts. Let's take time to REMEMBER what He has done, is doing and will do because of His great love and grace upon our lives. Giving Him thanks honors Him and brings us victory! Ps. 50:23 (She) who offers thank offerings honors Me, and (she) prepares the way so that I may show (her) the salvation of God.

_____

_____

_____

_____

Petition: (20 – 25 min.)

Father, help _____ to count all things as loss compared to the surpassing greatness of knowing Christ Jesus his/her Lord. Let _____gain Christ & be found in Him not having a righteousness that comes from the law, but that which is through faith in Christ—the righteousness that comes from God & is by faith. Philippians 3:7-9

My special and specific requests:

_____

_____

_____

_____

My thoughts and loving declarations:

_____

_____

_____

_____

Jehovah Rophe...Shepherd

Hello my name is Tangela Cullum, Granny, and I am writing this from the McPhcarson Women's Unit of Corrections in Newport, AR. I pray that you learn, just as I have that at times, the Shepherd must break the legs of the sheep in order to carry them on His shoulders. In doing this they not only learn the voice and love of their Father, but a stranger's voice they will NOT follow. I am in prison at this time living and learning this very precious truth. It's when the sheep's legs are broken that the relationship with his shepherd becomes intimately more personal. Prayer changes things! Oftentimes there is nothing that we can do for our loved ones or for our circumstances BUT pray! We also know that if we pray according to His will He hears us. It is His will not one of us should perish, but that everyone should have everlasting life. Know that as you pray for your grandchildren, children, and families the Shepherd hears the cries of His sheep's voice and tenderly leads them home.

Praise: (10-15 min.) Definition: **Jehovah Rophe** means God is my Shcphcrd; He leads us like sheep to pastures, water, out of danger, and to Himself. Shepherds fight for their flock and know their sheep individually (and they know his voice!). A shepherd is one who lives with his sheep!

A shepherd in real life stays with his sheep morning, noon, and night, never leaving them. Our God reminds us that He does the same with us, His sheep.

Scriptures : Psalm 23: 1; John 10:11 ; John 10: 14

Personal thoughts:

_____

_____

_____

_____

Confession: (2-3 silent min.)

Once we were like sheep that wandered away, but now you have turned to your Shepherd, the Guardian of your soul to confess your mistakes as well as your desire to return to Him and be restored. Grand friend, He hears! Jehovah Rophe restores my soul – Psalm 23: 3

Thanksgiving: (10-15 min.)

Psalm 73:24 My heart is full of thanks to the Lord for guiding me and my grandchildren with His counsel, leading us to a glorious destiny. How many thankful things can you list?

_____

_____

_____

_____

Petition: (20 – 25 min.)

Ezekiel 34:11 For this is what the Sovereign Lord (Jehovah Rophe) says: I, Myself, will search and find _____. I will be like a shepherd looking for His scattered flock. I will find _____ and rescue _____, I will bring _____ back home. I will tend _____ and give _____ a place to lie down in peace. I will search for _____ and will bring _____ safely home again. When _____ is injured I will bind his/her wounds, and when _____ is weak I will strengthen

_____.

My special and specific requests:

_____

_____

_____

_____

My thoughts and loving declarations:

_____

_____

_____

_____

Jehovah Shammah...There

What do I do when my grandchildren are far away and I can't hold them and tell them how much I love them each day? I can pray! AND I can pray calling on the name of Jehovah Shammah which means "The Lord is There." As their "Oma," even when I (Kendra Holden) cannot be there physically, I can trust that Jehovah Shammah *is* there. I have a granddaughter who is starting first grade this year. Having moved to a different city she is nervous about what to expect and about not having any friends in her new school. I 've been able to remind her of Joshua 1:9, "Be strong and courageous! Do not tremble or be dismayed, for the Lord your God is with you wherever you go." As much as I would like to be there with her to walk her through those first days, I can be assured that God *will* be there with her. What a comfort it is to know that He will never leave her or forsake her, that He is *always* there with her as Jehovah Shammah.

Praise: (10-15 min.)

Definition- **Jehovah Shammah**: Present, lovingly & powerfully available, ready to respond.

Scriptures where God promises His presence, that "He is there":

Josh.1:9; Ps.139:1-18; Matt.28:18-20; 1 Cor.3:16; Rev.21:3-4

Personal thoughts:

_____

_____

_____

_____

Confession (2-3 silent min.)

"If we confess our sins, He is faithful and just to forgive us our sins, and cleanse us from all unrighteousness." 1 Jn.1:9

Thanksgiving: (10-15 min.)

"...always giving thanks to God the Father for everything, in the name of the Lord Jesus Christ." Eph.5:20

_____

_____

_____

_____

Petition: (20 – 25 min.)

O God, Jehovah Shammah —I praise You that You are there with _____.

May he/she be strong and courageous because of the knowledge of Your presence in his/her life.

Bless _____ by making Your presence very real to him/her, and may he/she know that You have enclosed him/her behind and before, and laid Your hand on him/her.

(Based on scriptures used in PRAISE)

My special and specific requests:

_____

_____

_____

_____

My thoughts and loving declarations:

_____

_____

_____

_____

El Emunah...Faithful

It's me again, **says** our faithful God, who also calls Himself, El Emunah. In past years, I often looked at our sweet Old English Sheep Dog and thought, "My, but he's so faithful to look out for our daughters (ages 4 and 2). This very long-haired fun creature used to always love to follow along while I was pulling our girls in their red wagon along the dirt road! It wasn't long until Bart actually pulled the wagon with the girls inside, as I walked along beside! He seemed to take such pride in himself with the leather "get-up" we designed! Then as our daughters grew older, Bart stayed near their sides when playing out back or in a neighbor's yard. He relaxed near by, but kept watch over the children. I guess that's why these dogs are called Sheep Dogs. They are so faithful to watch over their little "sheep".

My name is G'ma Donna" Schroeder. You are invited to travel along with me to another beautiful reflection of our Father, EL MUNAH.

Praise: (10-15 min.)

Definition- **El Emunah**: Faithful God

Scriptures: Deuteronomy 7:9

"Therefore know that the LORD our God, He is God, the FAITHFUL God who keeps covenant and mercy for a thousand generations with those who love Him and keep His commandments."

God is also El Emunah, the faithful God of the past and the future. The Lord in Heaven knows all about you, thinks of you, and loves you. He is unlike an idol that can do nothing; who can't think, feel, or act. He will always keep His promises and His compassion is new every morning. How good is that? He so desires to share life with YOU, 24x7! You can speak to Him anytime of any day or night.

Personal thoughts:

_____

_____

_____

_____

Confession: (2-3 silent min.)

Quietly speak to El Emunah about how the rooms of your heart need a good   cleaning.

Have you been faithful to meet with Him daily? What displeases your faithful Father about your life? Grab the Clorox and be faithful to cleanse your heart now so that El Emunah can walk with you in all you do and will not turn His head and not hear because of any sin.

Lord, forgive me when I doubt and don't believe Your Word

 and its promises.

Thank You for reminding me that You are El Emunah, the Faithful God, who continually watches over me and my grands, and never lets us out of Your sight!

Thanksgiving: (10-15 min.)

Pour out your thanks to El Emunah for His faithfulness. Thank Him that He is able to help both you and your grandchildren walk confidently today because He so faithfully stands beside us.

El Emunah can be trusted to watch over our grandchildren, no matter how many miles distance you. Thank El Emunah for faithfully waiting to meet daily with both you and them in prayer.

How about also thanking Him for being faithful to punish (in love) any disobedience? Now, that's a tough one! Thanks for his Word and commandments and that he faithfully keep his Word – generation to generation. Thank Him for His mercy and that He is not yet "done" with your dear, <u>grand</u> children!

_____

_____

_____

_____

Petition: (20 – 25 min.)

This is a time of agreement with your faithful, El Emunah.

Scripture (taken from praise time) Deuteronomy 7:9

Therefore, may _____ know You, El Emunah, as his/her only God, and as his/her faithful, merciful God, who keeps every (covenant) promise for a thousand generations. May _____ cherish You and keep Your commandments always.

My special and specific requests:

_____

_____

_____

_____

My thoughts and loving declarations:

_____

_____

_____

_____

Jehovah Shalom...Peace

Greetings Grand Prayer Warriors! (If you're not a prayer warrior yet, you will be soon!) I jumped at the opportunity to worship God as Jehovah Shalom with you because that name is 'power-packed' with meaning!

Let me introduce myself and then I'll explain. My name is Jeannie Gibby: a "growing in numbers" grandma. I love to worship God, so I'm always looking for new revelation about His character and attributes. That's how I discovered the fuller, richer meaning of Shalom.

Get ready! Here's the Hebrew meaning of Shalom" (Drink-in each word slowly):

Peace, safety, prosperity, well-being, wholeness, complete health, tranquility, success, comfort, peace with your enemies on every side.

Wow! That's powerful! And friends, our Jehovah Shalom sent His son Jesus to die that we might know this peace that so describes Him, so let's praise Him!

Praise: (10-15 min.)

Definition- The God of Peace; Shalom= safe, well, happy, wealth, health, prosperity, and favor.

Scriptures- Numbers 6:24-26; Judges 6:23-24; Psalm 29:11; Psalm.119:165; John 14:27; Ephesians.2:14; Romans16:20

Take time to read each of these scriptures and write down the ways Jehovah Shalom is speaking to you about WHO He is!

Personal thoughts:

_____

_____

_____

_____

Confession: (2-3 silent min.)

Peace, shalom in your soul! Let the peace of God and the God of peace refresh you and replace all that is robbed or broken as you make this time your confession.

Let him make peace with Me, let him make peace with Me. Isaiah 27:5

Thanksgiving: (10-15 min.)

May this time of thanksgiving be a celebration of the peace that passes all understanding! Writing them down will bring the powerful remembrance now and often to silence the threat of peace.

Lord, you will establish peace for us, since You have also performed for us all our works. Isaiah 26:12

_____

_____

_____

_____

Petition: (20 – 25 min.)

The joy of speaking a blessing and a prayer over our grandchildren is our privilege. These words are like a blanket that wraps them up in the protective arms of our Jehovah Shalom.

The Lord bless _____ and keep him/her. The Lord make His face shine upon _____, and be gracious unto_____. The Lord lift up His countenance upon _____ and give him/her peace. (shalom) Num. 6:24-26

My special and specific requests:

_____

_____

_____

My thoughts and loving declarations:

_____

_____

_____

Jehovah Roi...God who sees

Nothing is hidden from the eyes of the Lord. Isn't that good news! We can never be out of His sight.

Hello! I am Meleah Runnells, and my grandmother name is MeMe. As I think back to a time when I wondered if God was 'seeing' what was going on in my life , one event I immediately go back to is when we received the news our son, and his girlfriend, were expecting our first grandchild. As we ask...where are you in this Lord...are you here...do you see? He QUICKLY answered a resounding YES! "I 'see' right where you are. I am fully aware of this trial you are in, and I am with you ALWAYS....just as I promised." As He walked with us through that time, we learned to embrace the place He had us, with a confident trust. ALL the things He intended to do in this trial, affected so many lives, in so many ways! We discovered we would not know Him so deeply unless we could experience His perfect 'insight' in circumstances like this because He uses them to refine us! He 'sees' far more than we do, as He looks deep into our hearts, and lives. It is only our Father that can bring about GOOD in it all. AND may I say that the "goodest" thing He brought to me that continues t be a reminder of His goodness is my granddaughter, Briley! (And I do mean GRAND!) What does HE want you to 'see' about Him today? Know that He sees *your* hurt, sees *your* struggle, He knows *your* heart and will not ever leave you. He walks with you too. Allow your gaze to focus upward to 'see' your Father's love and care for you.

Praise: (10-15 min.)Definition- The God who sees

Scriptures- Psalm 139; Psalm 34:15; Proverbs 15:3; Genesis 16:13;Job 34:21

Personal thoughts:

_____

_____

_____

_____

Confession: (2-3 silent min.)

When I realized that all my confessions were merely me telling the Lord what He already knew (because He is Jehovah Roi, the One who sees all), I was relieved. I understood my confession was more of an agreement with Him, rather than revealing anything new. And then to realize that even when He saw me in my guilt, my mistakes, or my shame and He loved me regardless! This is great news I just have to share. Come with me to the Throne of Grace, for He promises to forgive when we confess (what He already knows!)

The sacrifices of God are a broken spirit; a broken and contrite heart, O God You will not despise. Psalm 51:17

Thanksgiving: (10-15 min.)

Isaiah 11:3 "And he will delight in the fear of the LORD. He will not judge by what he **sees** with his eyes, or decide by what he hears with his ears;" but have confidence that the Lord 'sees' all. Share how you have learned to trust in what HE sees.

_____

_____

_____

_____

Petition: (20 – 25 min.)

Father, I ask that You give _____ the Counselor

to be with _____ forever. The world cannot accept

Him because it neither sees Him, nor knows Him, but

Father we ask that _____ will know You and

that Your Spirit will be in _____ and be

with him/her forever.

John 14: 16-18

My special and specific requests:

_____

_____

_____

_____

My thoughts and loving declarations:

_____

_____

_____

_____

Elohim – Creator God

Hi, I am Annette Watson (Nana) and I have an encouraging word about our Elohim, Creator God. My granddaughter, Katherine lost the vision in her left eye when she was a tiny baby. It took a long time and many prayer sessions with God for me to recognize that He has a redemptive purpose for everything He allows to come into our lives. Our Creator God had a marvelous plan for Katherine's life. I could never have imagined all the wonderful ways God would use this "flaw" in her to bring joy to her and glory to Himself.. One example is when she was on a mission trip to Honduras and was introduced to a young mother that had just been told her baby was blind in one eye. Kat was able to share with this sobbing mother how faithful God had been in her own life and encouraged her to trust God for her child. We have discovered that God has replaced Katherine's physical vision with deep spiritual insight. God has taught Kat to use her other four senses to compensate for the vision she does not have. She is a talented musician, outstanding student, honored athletic, natural leader and compassionate friend. Right now she is responding to God's call to her to live in Rwanda and share His love with the people there. God has proven His wisdom in allowing some difficulties in Kat's life in order to perfect the qualities He wanted for her. God shines as Creator and through his creations!

Praise: (10-15 min.)

Definition- **Elohim**: Creator God; all things begin with HIM!

Scriptures- Ps. 139:13-16; Genesis 1:27; Ephesians 2:10; Revelation 4:11

Personal thoughts:

_____

_____

_____

_____

Confession: (2-3 silent min.)

Our Creator God – Elohim – can see things even we cannot. Allow the One who has the master key go inside to help you clean up and remove anything that hinders your relationship with Him (or anyone else for that matter!)

Search me O God and know my heart; try me and know my anxious thoughts; and see if there is any hurtful way in me. AND lead me in the way everlasting. Psalm 139:24

Thanksgiving: (10-15 min.)

This time is always too short for me! I love to review all that the Lord is doing in my grandchildren's lives. His loving kindness is beyond my understanding, but not beyond my desire to remember and say thank you.

Give thanks to the God of Heaven, for His loving kindness is everlasting. Psalm 136:26

Petition: (20 – 25 min.)

Meditate on and pray these words with the One who inspired them: For _____ is His workmanship, created in Christ Jesus for good works, which God prepared beforehand so that _____ could walk in them. Ephesians 2:10

My special and specific requests:

_____

_____

_____

_____

My thoughts and loving declarations:

_____

_____

_____

_____

El Elyon...God Most High

As I reflect upon the first time I realized I would become a grandmother, the memory only grows sweeter though at that particular moment it was quite a shock! Funny how our Most High God works! Go back with me a minute and let's see together how He demonstrated just how high a Most High can be! I just happened to be in a prayer chapel a few minutes from home when my oldest daughter left a distressing phone message saying, "Mom, I need to see you right away." I knew I could both finish my commitment of time to pray and meet with her upon her immediate arrival in the time I had left. As I reviewed the serious sound of her voice, I was gripped with anticipation. At that moment in the chapel, it was as if the Lord, Himself whispered, "She's pregnant." It was just a short time later I heard those very words from her!   I simply embraced her shaking body and calmed her searching eyes with "I know, we will get through this." "The Lord prepared me." The days and prayers following focused on seeking the truth: truth about my daughter's relationship with her boyfriend, truth about the commitment of marriage, and the truth about this child being a wanted, created, treasure. I also had a friend who joined me in even asking our Most High for joy through it all, especially for this child to always know he was and is much loved. The day my first grandchild was born, I was in the room with my faithful friend and prayer partner and we were the first to see this baby born – WITH A

SMILE ON HIS FACE! May I say now, that I am a very proud Maw Maw of a teenager! His mom and dad married and have 3 more children. Now, can you rejoice with me that there is no high like the Most High!

Praise: (10-15 min.)

Definition- **EL ELYON:** Most High; higher than everyone and everything!

Scriptures- Psalm 9; Psalm 91:1, 2

Personal thoughts:

_____

_____

_____

_____

Confession: (2-3 silent min.)

Can a Most High God know every thought?   Can He see what is weighing us down, troubling us so, and separating me from Him?   There is no need to try hiding anything from the eyes of the Lord.   Allow the cleansing that comes with confession to bring refreshment to your heart and soul.

Let's confess and be made whole.

Thanksgiving: (10-15 min.)

Remember Psalm 9:2 from our praise time: "I will sing praise to Your Name, O Most High?" As you remember the many things your Most High God has done for your grandchildren, you will *want* to sing! The only hard part is to stop once you start!

_____

_____

_____

_____

Petition: (20 – 25 min.)

Our prayers are from one of the most popular psalms. These words are so comforting to hear and powerful to pray. Remember God's Word never returns void.

_____ , who dwells in the shelter of the Most High will abide in the shadow of the Almighty.

_____ will say to the Lord, "My refuge and my fortress." "My God in whom I trust." For He will give His angels charge concerning _____ , to guard _____ in all his/her ways.

Psalm 91: 1, 11

My special and specific requests:

_____

_____

_____

_____

My thoughts and loving declarations:

_____

_____

_____

_____

Jehovah Jireh...Provider

Jehovah means Provider. The Lord is my, Julia Kollmyer's, Provider! After raising four children and being blessed with 11 grandchildren, I decided I should start writing my thoughts, desires, and testimonies for them all to read long after I am gone. There is nothing like a written word which continues to speak! AND I have a lot to say! So, I began to write letters with a single focus, a profound truth, or just G'ma's advice. (I am G'ma to my grandchildren) All my letters seem to have one common denominator: God is their Jehovah Jireh. I boldly told them that God is THE source for their every need and though they may think they are pretty smart, unless they are seeking His wisdom, they will only get frustrated or even defeated. I also told them that their G'ma follows her own advice! How I hope and pray each of my grandchildren will grow in the knowledge and worship of their Provider as well as a good steward of all He provides.

Praise (Time: 10-15 minutes)

Definition-**Jehovah Jireh:** The Lord, My Provider (supplies, dispenses, bestows, pays for, equips, and delivers.)

Scriptures- Philippians. 4:19,20; Psalm 23:4;
Genesis 22:14; 2Corinthians 9: 6-11

Personal thoughts:

_____

_____

_____

_____

Confession: (2-3 silent min.)

What can be more profound than providing
forgiveness? Which one of us could say no to this
gift? Allow the intentions of Jehovah Jireh to restore
you to Himself by reviewing and rejecting everything
that separates you from Him.

For the sake of Your Name, Jehovah Jireh, forgive my
iniquity though it is great. Psalm 25:11

Thanksgiving: (10-15 min.)

When my oldest granddaughter needed money for college, she called me. We prayed over the phone asking for God's provision. Just a short time later, she called me again with the good news! Jehovah Jireh had provided! We wanted the world to know!

Give thanks to the Lord, call on His Name, Jehovah Jireh. Make known among the nations what He has done! Psalm 105:1

Petition: (20 – 25 min.)

Another phone call I received was from a teenage grandson who was so concerned about his father's health that he was in tears. I knew, though he did not ask, that he wanted me to pray with him for his dad to recover. We asked Jehovah Jireh together; a sweet time of surrender and a confirmation that he knew where and Who could provide the answer.

And God is able to make all grace abound to _____, so that in all things, at all times, having all things-_____ needs, _____ will abound in every good work. _____ will be made rich in every way so that _____ can be generous on every occasion which will result in thanksgiving to God.   2Corinthians 9:8

My special and specific requests:

_____

_____

_____

_____

My thoughts and loving declarations:

_____

_____

_____

_____

Jehovah Rapha...Healer

Honey is my name to my 7 grandboys. They know how important Jehovah Rapha is to me because they hear me quoting, "I have made you fearfully and wonderfully," as we pray *first* over hurts, wounds, and injuries of their little bodies, souls, or spirits. When one of my grandboys was born with a heart condition and underwent heart surgery only 10 days old, we all called on Jehovah Rapha for His mercy, grace, and will to heal this most loved little boy. Nahum 1:7 says, "I am good, a refuge in times of trouble." As I prayed these words I felt a growing peace and comfort that healing is in His hands, after all it is His Name: Jehovah Rapha, and it is His mark, His character, and His powerful, mysteriously wonderful identity.

I have enjoyed carrying notecards with meaningful verses, especially healing scriptures on them so that I can pray for my children and grandchildren. One day I will give them these cards with the dates and descriptions so that they can be reminded of the power and faithfulness of Jehovah Rapha. Join me in leaving this legacy.

Praise: (10 – 15 min.)

Definition- **Jehovah Rapha:** God, My Healer – Thaumaturge – the unrivaled worker of wonders and miracles!

Scriptures- Psalm 139: 14-17; Psalm 136: 4; Nahum 1:7 Psalm 9:9,10; Psalm 34: 19-22

Personal Thoughts:

_____

_____

_____

_____

Confession (2-3 silent min.)

If I regard iniquity in my heart, the Lord will not hear me; But verily God hath heard me; He hath attended to my voice in prayer. Blessed be God, which hath not turned away my prayer or His mercy from me. Psalm 68:18-20

This is the perfect time to confess all the heaviness in your heart to a forgiving God. His Word is true, His forgiveness is sure, and His mercy is personal and powerful.

Thanksgiving: (10-15 min.)

Unto Thee, O God, do we give thanks, unto Thee do we give thanks; for that Thy name is near thy wondrous works declare.

Psalms 75:1

Thy works of healing declare the wonders of our God. Healing physically, mentally, emotionally, or spiritually is in the Hands of our God. Let us thank Him. We can even thank Him before we *see* the results

_____

_____

_____

_____

Petition: (20 – 25 min.)

As we proclaim God's Word, let us broaden our concept of His healing to include every possible need our grandchildren may have (wounded spirits, broken hearts, ailing bodies, or troubled minds.) Jehovah Rapha's healing is deep, thorough, and forever. Jehovah Rapha's healing is deep, thorough, and forever.

Many are the afflictions of _____, my righteous one, but the Lord delivereth _____ out of all his/her troubles.

He keepeth all _____'s bones; not one of them is broken.

Evil shall slay the wicked; and they that hate the righteous shall be desolate.

The Lord redeemeth the soul of _____ and none of them that trust in Him shall be desolate.   Psalm 34: 19-22

My special and specific requests:

My thoughts and loving declarations:

Jehovah Nissi...Banner

Granny here! I have another name, too! It is Tangela Cullum and I am a grandmother of 6 (and counting!) Currently I am in a State Detention Center in the Arkansas. My life is changing daily because of prayer and I am most thankful for the chance to pray for my grandchildren, but more than that - to offer an invitation for you to join me. Our God is teaching me daily that His banner over me is love and I haven't messed up too much, missed Him or His will just because I am separated from my babies. I can wave this same banner WITH Him over them by praying His Word. He has made me a grandmother and I am honored to carry the standard, His flag, into battle for those I love so dearly. There is victory in Jehovah Nissi, My Banner; only in Him, do I triumph!

Praise: (Time: 10 –15 minutes)

Definition: Jehovah Nissi means God is my Banner; The One who waves His flag and claims you and me as His. He delivers and saves and gives the victory! The Miracle Maker, my banner of redemption to be held high for all to see.

Scriptures : Song of Solomon 2:4; Psalms 60:4; Psalms 20:5-8;Isaiah 11:10

Personal Thoughts:

_____

_____

_____

_____

Confession: (Time: 2-3 silent minutes)

    For He must reign until He has put all enemies under His feet. 1Corinthians 15:25

My confessed sins are under His feet and He reigns !

Lord, I confess I have not always stood under your banner. I have sought victory in and through my own strengths and abilities – and even through other people and things. As I let you search my heart. Make them clear to me, so I can agree with You and surrender them to You. I pray now, Lord, for your forgiveness and I ask you to please make Your name, Jehovah Nissi, known to me.

Thanksgiving: (Time: 10-15 minutes)

I thank You, Jehovah Nissi, right now for Your deliverance and victory. And I thank You for these victories in my grandchildren's lives:

_____

_____

_____

_____

Petition :_(Time: 20 –25 minutes)_

Psalm 20: We will sing for joy over _____'s victory. And in the Name of Jehovah Nissi, we set up our banner. May the Lord fulfill all _____'s petitions. Now, I know the Lord saves _____, His anointed. He will answer _____ from His holy heaven with the saving strength of His right hand. _____ trusts in Jehovah Nissi, the name of the Lord _____'s God.

My special and specific requests:

_____

_____

_____

_____

My thoughts and loving declarations:

_____

_____

_____

_____

Names of Jesus

Light

Bread

Door

Love

Same Yesterday, Today, and
Tomorrow

Lamb of God

Good Shepherd

Savior

Friend

Teacher

True Vine

Intercessor

The Good Shepherd

Sheep—they are the dumbest of animals! I (Kendra Holden), grew up with sheep, and know first hand how dumb they are. They follow the sheep in front of them, regardless of where they are going, and get into all kinds of trouble because of it. They are easy prey for their enemies, and scatter when they are afraid. They *need* a shepherd! God likens us to sheep over and over again in the Scriptures—and says that we have a "good Shepherd", Jesus. As "Oma", I can already see my little grandchildren looking at the bright lights and sounds of the world, and I cry out to their "good Shepherd" to call their names and protect them from those who would prey on their hearts and minds. I can trust Him to care for these little lambs, to carry them close, because He is a *good* Shepherd...

Praise: Jesus our Good Shepherd

(Time: 10-15 minutes)

Definition: One who lives with his sheep (not just cares for them); a leader, protector

Scriptures about our "Good Shepherd":

Psalm 23; Isaiah 40:11; Matthew 18:11-14; John 10:7-16, 27-29; Revelation 7:16-17

Personal Thoughts:

_____

_____

_____

_____

Confession: (2-3 minutes)

"I will confess my transgressions to the LORD..."
Ps.32:5

Thanksgiving: (10-15 min.)

"Always giving thanks to God the Father for everything, in the name of the Lord Jesus Christ."
Eph.5:20

_____

_____

_____

_____

Petition: (based on scripture used in praise time)

"Dear Jesus, our Good Shepherd, I thank you for the promise that Your sheep *will* hear Your voice! May _____ know You, and follow You as his/her shepherd, and in turn know the abundant life that You have for him/her." John 10: 10, 16

My special and specific requests:

_____

_____

_____

_____

My thoughts and loving declarations:

_____

_____

_____

_____

The Same -yesterday, today and forever

Ponder that for a moment. There is only One in all of history whom we can count on to be the same each day, month, year, and through eternity, and it is Christ Jesus! I sit by the window at our computer and look out at the fresh 10 inches of snow left in Colorado just a day ago. How large the fluffy white flakes were as they fell to the ground! Can you believe that I can already see the brown earth, and tracks going everywhere? One day our grandchild starts kindergarten and much too soon its graduation time.

Life is so full of changes, good and bad. Perhaps it's our health, attitudes towards us, or even planned activities. Can you think of anything or anyone that does NOT change? God's word says that our precious Jesus NEVER changes. He alone is the same yesterday, today, and forever, as is His Word and His love for us! Thank you sweet Jesus!

Donna Schroeder – better known as Nana or G'Ma Donna!

Praise: Jesus, the SAME - Yesterday, Today and Forever!

(Time: 10-15 minutes)

Definition: Jesus never changes, He remains as He was, is, and will be!

Scripture: Hebrews 13:8

Does this remind you of another name for the Father? Is it YAHWEH?

Jesus is the Beginning and the End, so praise Him that He'll not lead you for a while and then forsake you. He alone can give you peace such as He did for Noah and Joshua at Jericho. Yesterday is gone and tomorrow is not yet here. We praise Him that He is the One who can positively change our todays and each day after because of the fact HE remains constant as the One who DOES NOT CHANGE!

Personal Thoughts:

_____

_____

_____

_____

Confession: (Time: 2-3 minutes)

Lord, as a Grandmother, I desire to place the past under Your blood. Please forgive my sins as I commit my future to You. Forgive my times of weakness when I don't have the courage to face the future. Forgive those times when I did not do things in Your will, Your way, and in Your timing, but my own!

Thanksgiving: (Time: 10-15 minutes)

In this incredible time when it seems that nothing stays the same for even a minute, thank Jesus for being your Rock. Let your heart flow with ways you desire to thank Him for those around you and that they are in His care eternally. Thank Him for their faith and the truth that they can live for Jesus today.

_____

_____

_____

_____

Petition: (Time: 20-25 minutes)

Grace and peace to _____ from Him who is, and who was, and who is to come and from the seven spirits before His throne, and from Jesus Christ who is the faithful witness, the firstborn from the dead and the ruler of the kings of the earth. Jesus, who loves _____ and has freed _____ from sin by His blood and has made _____ to be a kingdom and priest to serve His God and Father,. To Him be glory and power for ever and ever. Amen. Revelation 1:4-5

My special and specific requests:

_____

_____

_____

_____

My thoughts and loving declarations:

_____

_____

_____

_____

My Intercessor

　　While spending the night with my young grandgirls, they invited me to jump in the middle of them at bedtime. As we snuggled down after saying our prayers and singing a few of their favorite songs, it got very quiet. I was tempted to turn my head and peek at my oldest, Barrett, checking to see if she was already asleep. Nope, she was wide awake. She looked back at me and said, "MeMe, I am just talking to God about you." It shocked me so, I was speechless. Nothing more was said between us then as she drifted off to sleep, yet I still remember the humbling impact of those words from an innocent, four-year-old, and "precious to me" little girl. (And I thought I was the one who talked to God about her!)

When we talk to God about our grandchildren, we are following the example of Jesus – Intercessor. He talks to God about us! He lives to talk to God about us!

Isn't it wonderful to know we have Jesus as our always and forever prayer partner?

I am Caryn Southerland – MeMe, to my grandgirls!

Praise: Jesus, My Intercessor

(Time: 10-15 minutes)

Definition: Jesus takes my needs (problems, desires, diseases, weaknesses, hopes, etc) to the Father – everyone, everyday! . He cares enough to carry us by being on His knees in prayer for our grandchildren and us! He knows what to say and how to say it so that the answer will result in blessing us and bonding us to Him. He wants to teach us by holding our hands. He cares enough to carry us by being on His knees in prayer for our grandchildren and us.

Scripture: Hebrews 7: 25; Job 16: 19-21; John 17: 9, 15 -17, 20 −25

Personal Thoughts:

_____

_____

_____

_____

Confession: (Time: 2-3 minutes)

Lord Jesus, when I confess my sins I am no longer separated from You. Your prayer to sanctify me by the truth of God's word is my affirmation that you want me to come to You no matter how much I feel unclean or unworthy. By my confession I am invited back into close fellowship with You and the joy of being completely restored. I will confess my transgressions to the Lord, and you forgave the guilt of my sin. Psalm 32:5.

Thanksgiving :(Time: 10-15 minutes)

Just the thought of having Jesus lead the prayer time your grandchild is enough to make you shout and rejoice. We know He knows "how" to pray and "what" the real need is for our grandchildren. So we can offer thanks to Him for the many ways we hear or watch our grandchildren receive the rewards of those prayers. Our thanks to Him is a celebration and a wonderful way to acknowledge His faithful outpouring of every good and perfect gift at the perfect time and in the perfect way for those "becoming perfections" of ours!

_____

_____

_____

_____

Petition: (Time: 20-25 minutes)

John 17:24-25
(Jesus teaches to pray as He prayed. These are His
words spoken to His Father for His disciples, "the
ones given Him" We can pray these same words for
those the Father has given us)

Father, I want my grandchild,_____ to be with

Jesus wherever He is. And to see the glory of Jesus.

Righteous Father, I agree with Jesus that He has

made You known to _____ (by coming to this

earth, dying on the cross, and being resurrected) and

Jesus will continue to make You known (through the

Word and Your Spirit) in order that the love You gave

Jesus for _____ may be in _____

and that Jesus, Himself, may be in

_____.

My special and specific requests:

_____

_____

_____

_____

My thoughts and loving declarations:

_____

_____

_____

_____

Friend

Hello, Fellow Grandmothers. I am Bernadette Post, fondly called B by my sweetie grandgirls. As I think of the friendship I long for with my grandgirls and future grandchildren, focusing on Jesus as Friend is very fitting in our lives. It is because Jesus loves us as Friend that we are able to share a friendship with our grandchildren. He is the one that gives us the grace and teaches us to LOVE and to be FRIEND to them. We have a special place in their lives because we can even share things with them that at times it is even difficult for their parents to share with them. So as you ponder on Jesus our Friend, embrace his PERSONAL friendship in your own life and pass on that legacy of Jesus as Friend to your grandchildren.

Praise: Jesus as FRIEND

(Time: 10-15 minutes)

Definition:. Real friendship looks at the heart, not just the "packaging." Genuine friendship loves for love's sake, not just for what it can get in return. True friendship is both challenging and exciting. It risks, it overlooks faults, and it loves unconditionally, but it also involves being truthful, even though it may hurt.

Scriptures: John 15:12-15; Job 29:4;   John 14: 27; Exodus 33:11; James 2:23

Personal Thoughts:

_____

_____

_____

_____

Confession: (Time: 2-3 minutes)

And Jesus is gentle as he shares truths in our lives that we need to have revealed to us so that we might change and become more like Him. He faithfully forgives us (just as a friend would) when we make our sins, shortcomings, and failings known to Him through our confession.

Thanksgiving: (Time: 10-15 minutes)

Genuine friendship, also called "agape" love, comes from the Lord. The Lord Jesus calls us His friends and He laid down His life for us (John 15). That is the ultimate LOVE that He laid down his life for us. And that He sees fit to call us friend. Through this personal friendship and relationship with Him, He gives us the grace to befriend others and share who He is with those He places in our lives. Let's thank Him for the many ways He shows us this truth!

_____

_____

_____

_____

Petition: (Time: 20-25 minutes)

I pray (as Jesus commands) that
_____would know the meaning of these
words in his/her life: Love each other as I have loved
you, _____.

Greater love has no one than this, that he lay down
his life for his friends.

You, _____, are my friend if you do what I
command. I no longer call you servant, because a
servant does not know his master's business.

Instead, I have called you friend, _____.

For everything that I learned from my Father I have
made known to _____.   (John 15: 12-1)

My special and specific requests:

_____

_____

_____

_____

My thoughts and loving declarations:

_____

_____

_____

_____

The Lamb

In days of old, an innocent lamb was used as a sacrificial offering. God's mercy sent His One and only Son, Jesus, THE perfect Lamb to be our sacrifice when we choose to believe and receive Him.

Sweet little 'lamb' climb into my lap- REST, BE PROTECTED, KNOW LOVE. We love scooping up our precious ones to hold closely and talk. Well, so does our Heavenly Father!

My name is Meleah Runnells, also known as "MeMe". God has some love and redemption to share with us today through **Jesus the Lamb,** our perfect and eternal sacrifice.

Praise: Jesus, the Lamb of God

(Time: 10-15 minutes)

Definition - sacrificial, atonement for sin.

Scriptures - Leviticus 5:5; I Corinthians 5:6-8; Luke 22:7-20; Revelations 5:1-14

Personal Thoughts:

_____

_____

_____

_____

Confession: (Time: 2-3 minutes)

In this time of quiet solitude allow the Spirit to examine your heart. The Savior's blood will cleanse you, as you recognize and repent of those things that keep you 'pinned' back from Him. Allow Him to look deeply and make you aware of your sin. He only exposes what He wants to redeem. Give Him the freedom to bring that purity to your heart again today. Behold, _____(your name) the Lamb of God who has taken away the sin of the world! (and your sin) John 1:29

Thanksgiving:

The Lord always provides for His little lambs. Share how you have seen His provision for your 'little lamb' this week.

_____

_____

_____

_____

Petition: Psalm 100:3

As we place our 'lambs' before the throne we assured of His love and good plans for them. Pray that they too will know the **Lamb of God.**

May_____ know that the Lord is God that He has made him/her and he/she is His.

May _____ always know that the Lord is good and that His love endures forever.

My special and specific requests:

_____

_____

_____

_____

My thoughts and loving declarations:

_____

_____

_____

_____

Love

When my grandson James was two years old someone gave him a C/D of original Christian songs. Now, he had been given lots of musical C/Ds but for some reason this one immediately caught his attention. James began to lift up his arms and sway to the music and he would listen to the songs over and over again. He was actually worshipping God even though his little mind could not possibly understand the theological truth he was hearing. James has Down Syndrome and at two years old, his mental development was at an 8-15 month level and yet, there was no doubt that the words about Jesus and His love were reaching his little spirit. He did not know one Bible verse but somehow he knew Jesus and experienced God's love to give us His son, Jesus who lived and died to represent His depth of that love. Perhaps, this is the message that rang clearly and often in James' ears; he insisted on listening to that C/D everyday for about two years! He finally memorized each song and still sings them with the passion we all would like to have for Jesus. I am Annette Watson to the world, but I am Nanna to James and so excited to be his grandmother. James and Jesus make a great team as they teach me that Jesus knows exactly how to communicate to each one of us that He loves us in the most intimate way.

Praise: Jesus is Love

(Time: 10-15 min.)

Definition – the action of God the Father's heart for each of us: to send His only son with the sacrificial message that proves His constant and adamant activity of caring for all He has made.

Scriptures – Romans 5:8; 1John 4:7-10; Romans 8:37-39; 1John 4:16-19

Personal Thoughts:

_____

_____

_____

_____

Confession: (Time: 2-3 minutes)

It was love that took Jesus to the cross to be whipped, beaten, and demeaned for each one of us. It was love that poured out in the form of blood to cover every wrong past, present, and future. And it IS love now that calls us to give up our sin and shame, lay down our guilt, and confess our shortcomings so that we can embrace and be embraced by the love that conquers, covers, and cleanses us. Love covers all transgressions. Proverbs 10:12

Thanksgiving: (Time: 10-15 min.)

We give thanks to You, O God, we give thanks. For Your Name is near. Psalm 75:1 This is a fun time of offering thanks to a loving Lord as you remember the many things He is doing or has recently done.

_____

_____

_____

_____

Petition: (20 – 25 min.)

Love can be both a noun and verb here. What a powerful word to pray for your grandchildren! Made in the image of God, we can pray boldly for that image to be an ever and ongoing process within our grandchildren:

_____ is patient, _____ is kind and is not jealous. _____does not brag and is not arrogant.

_____does not act unbecomingly;

_____does not seek his/her own,

_____ is not provoked, or take into account a wrong suffered. _____does not rejoice in unrighteousness, but rejoices with the truth.

_____bears all things, believes all things, hopes all things, endures all things.

_____never fails because he/she is full of the love of God. 1 Corinthians 13:4-8

My special and specific requests:

_____

_____

_____

_____

My thoughts and loving declarations:

_____

_____

_____

_____

Savior

GiGi here! (Cindy Rush) The name my grandchildren will cry when they need a human savior! I love hearing them call my name, even when it is when they are desperate for something denied, in trouble, or frantically fearful! Walking in these grand shoes have allowed me to relate to Jesus on a deeper level as I realize the power, privilege and joy of rescuing my little girls. Is this my purpose? In part, perhaps; I also know part of my purpose is to use these situations to point them to Jesus by saying, "Jesus is 100 times better and bigger than GiGi!"

As a grandmother, I am growing in appreciation for the passion and purpose Jesus had when He came to earth as the One who would offer salvation through His sacrifice. He came to show the heart of the Father and offer salvation to me, my grandchildren, and each of you and your grandchildren. How I want to use my influence to transfer this truth and watch my little legacies understand their great need for a Savior beyond their GiGi . Today our prayers line up with the intent of the Father, the mission of Jesus, and the reason the Holy Spirit remains. Let's get to work!

Isn't it a blessing worth waiting for to have grandchildren ?

Praise: Jesus is Savior

(Time: 10-15 minutes)

Definition – Overwhelming powerful love with a mission: to bring us to the Father as believers and followers of His only begotten son, Jesus.

Scriptures – 1John 4:14, 15; John 3:16, 17; John 14:1-3; Luke 15:3-7

Personal Thoughts:

_____

_____

_____

_____

Confession: (Time: 2-3 minutes)

Oh Lord, the one who hears prayer; we all arrive at your doorstep sooner or later, loaded with guilt. Our sins are too much for us, but You get rid of them once and for all. (Psalm 65:2 The Message) Jesus knew we needed a Savior with an ear to hear and a heart to forgive. This is our time to stop, take a look at that load, admit your guilt, and surrender them to Jesus.

A Savior can best save when there is cooperation!

Thanksgiving: (Time: 10-15 minutes)

Come and see the works of God, who is awesome in His deeds toward the sons of men. Come and hear, all who fear God and I will tell of what He has done for my soul.! (Psalm 66: 5,16)

Looking back for the many times your Savior made Himself known in this powerful name is a great treasure hunt! Enjoy the dig!

_____

_____

_____

_____

Petition: (20 – 25 min.)

This is such a familiar verse, perhaps the first one you ever memorized. May these words be refreshed, renewed, and magnified in your mind and heart as you pray them now with your grandchildren's names filling the blanks.

For God so loved _____, that He gave

His only son, Jesus, that _____ should

believe in Him, should not perish but have everlasting

life. John 3:16

My special and specific requests:

_____

_____

_____

_____

My thoughts and loving declarations:

_____

_____

_____

_____

Teacher

Jesus, my teacher, is especially special to me. I'm Cindy Stockdale and I got my degree in early childhood education only to have a brief career as a teacher because four daughters permanently interrupted me! Though I have utilized my degree in the practical sense, I find myself as a perpetual student! Truthfully, I have stayed in Jesus' classroom so that I could pass on to my girls what I seemed to be constantly learning from Him. Do we ever stop learning! Now as a Mimi to my seven (and counting) grandchildren, I value even more this privilege of using these spiritual lessons (past, present, and future.) I am challenged with the fast pace of today and the competition of Internet, television, and other resources available to our younger ones. Yet, with all those, there is nothing that can compare with a simple sunset to set the scene for an exercise in the majesty of our Father God. Just recently three of my grandchildren spent Palm Sunday weekend with us. It was the perfect time to discuss the resurrection story using plastic eggs filled with ordinary things that help explain the following Easter Sunday: the death and new life of Jesus. Their faces were priceless as we got to the empty egg. "He is not here? He is alive? Jesus is alive! Yea, Jesus!" We tucked each one in singing our favorite bedtime song for three generations now: "Jesus, Jesus, Jesus", there's just something about that name! Amen!

Jesus taught using everyday events as object lessons, examples, and parables to transfer kingdom wisdom, so can we! Don't you feel we are holding hands with Jesus in this very important name as teacher?   Let's praise and pray together as He is our timeless, faithful, forever teacher.

Praise: Rabboni, Jesus second name!

(Time: 10-15 minutes)

Definition: one who has knowledge to transfer to others; instructor, mentor, coach.

Scripture: John 3:1–7; John 8: 1-11; John 13:13-15; John 20: 10-18; Matthew 7: 24-29; Mark 12: 35-37; Luke 7: 40-43

Personal Thoughts:

_____

_____

_____

_____

Confession: (Time: 2-3 minutes)

All teachers know that "time out" is valuable for arresting a situation! We can willingly seat ourselves in the timeout chair and confess our troubles and woes. The result from this time with our Teacher is always restoration, rejuvenation, and a re-energized spirit . His desire is not to condemn, but to transform through forgiveness and prepare us to accept on going training. (Remember the woman caught in adultery? John 8: 1-11)

Thanksgiving: (Time: 10-15 minutes)

Psalm 86: 11-12 Teach me, Your way, O Lord; I will walk in your truth. Unite my heart to fear Your name. I will give thanks to You, O Lord, my God with all my heart! And glorify Your name forever. Make your grateful list of things your grandchildren have learned or things you observe they are learning now so that one day you both can celebrate and glorify His name, Teacher, forever!

_____

_____

Petition: (Time: 20-25 minutes)

All authority in heaven and earth has been given to Me. Therefore _____, go and make disciples of all nations, baptizing them in the name of the Father, Son, and Holy Spirit and teaching them to obey everything I have commanded you. And surely I am with _____ always, to the end of the age. Matthew 28:18-19

My special and specific requests:

_____

_____

_____

_____

My thoughts and loving declarations:

_____

_____

_____

_____

The True Vine

How I can relate to this name of Jesus! Because I am the wife of a chef and I, too, love to cook and entertain; it seems much about our life has revolved around the food ! As I read and reread John 15 about Jesus being the true vine, God, the Father as our Gardner, it speaks volumes to spiritual soul. All too well I have experienced the beauty, purpose, and blessing of the goodness of the "vine." Staying connected to the life-giving source is key! My four grandsons know that every Sunday it is lunch at Nana's. We have a table especially built for our large and growing family and sitting down for a meal after church on our Sabbath is my joy to prepare for that purpose of connecting as a family and to our Lord. Every chance I have to invite them over for special projects like making gingerbread houses at Christmas, we have the chance to connect even more. I can show them as well as tell the about Jesus as we build relationships. My forever prayer for my grandchildren is that they would produce fruit, learn to endure the pruning process, and abide in the One who gives them life. I want to use my gifts and position as grandmother to encourage each one to accept, love, and live for Jesus. Sincerely, Nancy Bingham, also Nana!

Praise: Jesus, the True Vine

(Time: 10-15 minutes)

Definition: life receiver from the master gardener, life giver to the branches, the one who is true in comparison to other vines, the source of significance for life.

Scripture: John 15 : 1-11

Personal Thoughts:

_____

_____

_____

_____

Confession: (Time: 2-3 minutes)

John 15: 2 & 3 Pruning and cleansing is part of the growth process. When it is likened to confession, we can easily experience the necessity of letting go of our bad habits, wrong thoughts, and worthless activities. Jesus, our true vine, reminds us that His words clean us as we read them because they correct and replace bad habits, thoughts and activities with life giving truth. Jesus gave us His life, paid for each of those so that we can remain attached with the ultimate flow of goodness from Him to us. Enjoy this time as Jesus lops off the unnecessary and opens up the gate of grace to forgive, cleanse, and restore. Fruit is just around the corner!

Thanksgiving: (Time: 10-15 minutes)

What do you say to someone who lays His life down in exchange of yours, calls you his friend, promises you answers to your prayers. THANKS would be a great start!   Join me in remembering the many things our Jesus provided as He lived, just last week and provides today. Feel the connection of real relationship building as you do.   John 15:13-16

_____

_____

_____

_____

Petition: (Time: 20-25 minutes)

I am the vine, _____ is the branch.

_____ that abideth in Me and I in

_____ the same bringeth forth much fruit;

for without Me, _____ can do nothing.

_____ has not chosen Me, but I have chosen

_____ and ordained _____ that

_____shall go forth and bring forth fruit,

fruit that should remain; that whatsoever

_____ shall ask of the Father in My name,

He may give it to you.   John 15: 5,16

My special and specific requests:

_____

_____

_____

_____

My thoughts and loving declarations:

_____

_____

_____

_____

The Light of the World

The call came just as I was stepping in my front door. It was my son needing my assistance in picking up his younger daughter, the youngest of my 7 grandchildren. Available is my middle name; my first is MeMaw! Ha! When I arrived at the school and spotted my "joy" she met me with a huge knowing smile that I was the lucky one to pick her up. As we walked to the car I commented on her "outfit" which was very interesting to me. She has always been an artistic child in every way so I asked her about how she chose her clothes for that day. She simply said she just wanted to put on **everything** that was her favorite – in the dark! Her knee high boots were unzipped immediately after she locked her seatbelt. With a confused expression and a tilted head, she questioned out loud the fact her feet were hurting. Then we laughed! We realized she had been wearing them on the wrong feet!

The light is essential for getting it right! How many times I feel "in the dark" or its effects of discomfort or even pain! As I was thinking about how to relate this experience with my granddaughter I realized: Jesus is MY Light. He allows me (us) full expression of who I am (I can wear ALL my favorite things) AND at the same time, He can save me the painful "wrong feet" experiences! Prayer is like the light switch! When I come to Him in prayer, He en**lightens** me. Join me, Carolyn Hardie, in praying for our grandchildren to be flooded with Jesus, the Light of the world.

Praise: Jesus, the Light of the World

(Time: 10-15 minutes)

Definition: light brings life, warmth, and illumination. Light is not just the absence of darkness; it is the presence of God, Jesus, and Holy Spirit.

Scripture: John 1: 1-5; Revelation 21: 22-24; John 12: 35, 36, 46; John 8:12; 1st John 1:5-7

Personal Thoughts:

_____

_____

_____

_____

Confession: (Time: 2-3 minutes)

1ˢᵗ John 1:7 says that if we walk in the light, as He is in the light, we have fellowship with one another, and the blood of Jesus, His Son, purifies us from ALL sin. We can pause with cooperation to confess everything from "whoops" to purposeful "wrong" and allow the blood of Jesus to make us clean before the Father. Our agreement, then acceptance of forgiveness, and receiving the full restoration is one way to walk in the light.

Thanksgiving: (Time: 10-15 minutes)

We have been given the opportunity to experience the "LIGHT of life." Jesus brings life with His light – abundance, answered prayer, fresh promises, real protection, restored health, a phone call, a hug! Remember them; list them; and thank Him!

_____

_____

_____

_____

Petition: (Time: 20-25 minutes)

Matthew 5: 14-16

_____ is the light of the world. A city on a hill cannot be hidden. Neither do people light a lamp and put it under a bowl. Instead they put it on its stand and it gives light to everyone in the house. In the same way, let _____ 's light shine before men, that they may see _____'s good deeds and praise _____'s Father in heaven.

My special and specific requests:

_____

_____

_____

_____

My thoughts and loving declarations:

_____

_____

_____

_____

The Bread of Life

JESUS, THE BREAD OF LIFE.....WOW!, JESUS, the necessity, the sustenance that gives everlasting, eternal life to everyone who eats the bread He offers. JESUS, is the living bread that came down out of heaven. JESUS, the food, lovingly given by Father God, so that we may live forever with Him. JESUS, is the bread of life. JESUS, is the life giver!

Hi I'm MiMi, at least that is what my precious grandbabies, Callie, Riley and Addison call me. To everyone else I'm Kathy Pearson. It is so awesome to think of our precious Jesus as the BREAD OF LIFE.

He is the One Who gives us everything we need! He saved us from sin and death, gave us eternal life the moment we received Him as the nourishment we so desperately needed. He fills us to overflowing with His unconditional love, and guides and leads us in that love. Just the mention of the name of Jesus, calms our souls.

I remember when Callie was just an infant, I would rock her and sing to her to help her calm down and fall asleep. It never failed, when I would sing "Jesus Loves Me This I Know, for the Bible tells me so. Little ones to Him belong. We are weak, but He is strong. Yes, Jesus loves me! Yes, Jesus loves me! Yes, Jesus loves me! The Bible tells me so." Callie would calm down and she would stare at me with the most peaceful look on her sweet face. The very mention of the name Jesus calmed her. I can't wait to tell her, and Riley and Addison and my future grandbabies, more about Jesus, THE BREAD OF LIFE!!

God loves each one of our little ones so much; He doesn't want us to leave any of them out!!!! We grandmothers truly do have an awesome privilege to share about Jesus and pray for each sweet life the Lord puts in our life.

Praise: Jesus, the Bread of Life

(Time: 10-15 minutes)

Definition: bread is the most basic of food for our bodies and Jesus as our Bread of Life is the most basic for our souls!

Scripture: John 6: 48-51, 56-58

Personal Thoughts:

_____

_____

_____

_____

Confession: (Time: 2-3 minutes)

Come boldly to the throne of grace and confess anything that separates you from the Father. Jesus, THE BREAD OF LIFE, gives us access to meet with Him! Hebrews 4:16 So let us, grandmothers, come boldly to the throne of our gracious God. There we will receive His mercy, and we will find grace to help us when we need it. Hebrews 12:1 Grandmothers, let us strip off every weight that slows us down, especially the sin that so easily hinders our progress. And let us run with endurance the race that God has set before us.

Thanksgiving: (Time: 10-15 minutes)

Psalm 100:4-5 (Grandmothers), enter His gates with thanksgiving; go into His courts with praise. Give thanks to Him and bless His name. (Grandmothers) The Lord is good. His unfailing love continues forever, and His faithfulness continues to each generation.

_____

_____

_____

Petition: (Time: 20-25 minutes)

John 6:50-51..... The BREAD from heaven gives
eternal life to_____ as he/she eats it. Jesus is
the living BREAD that came down out of heaven.
As_____ eats this BREAD _____ will
live forever; this BREAD is My flesh, offered so
_____ may LIVE!

My special and specific requests:

_____

_____

_____

_____

My thoughts and loving declarations:

_____

_____

_____

_____

The Door

Revelation 3:20 "I stand at the door and knock. If anyone hears my voice and opens the door, I will come in and eat with him, and him with me"!

One of my favorite times as a grandmother is when my twin granddaughters Rhealea and Marlea come for a visit to their "D.D.'s" house. They ring the doorbell and are usually peering through the glass as I approach the door. As soon as I open it, they are both showing me their "new" things, like necklaces, bracelets, or even new sandals. These visits are a delight to me, and each visit is like a tiny glimpse of heaven--with two little angels!

Being a grandmother is a growing delight as I currently have a total of four with two more on the way.   Praying for each one helps me stay connected since I don't get to see them as often as I would like. And praying the Word assures me that these prayers stick!

Those faces at my door remind me that Jesus, Our Door, enables us to delight our Father God when we DO pray, (come to Him with our triumphs and trials.) We knock on His Door as we pray in Jesus' Name. Can you hear Him say, COME IN, I have been waiting for you!

Praise: Jesus IS the Door to the Father)

(Time: 10-15 minutes)

Definition: doors are the opening, gateways, portals in which you enter; doors allow passage both in and out; doors are absolutely necessary; though small in comparison, doors led to large places.

Scriptures: John 10: 1-9; John 14: 1-6

Personal Thoughts:

_____

_____

_____

_____

Confession: (Time: 2-3 minutes)

Jesus, our Door, allows us access to our Father God so that we can personally confess our sins rather than sacrifice an animal or have a priest confess for us. Let us receive this invitation from the Father and through Jesus let us unload our heavy burdens of guilt, shame, and disappointment in ourselves. The Door is open. Confess them!

Hear the forgiveness, feel the freedom, and receive the refreshment in the Father's lap just beyond the Door.

Thanksgiving: (Time: 10-15 minutes)

Time to celebrate! The door is open for the exchange of heartfelt thanks for the gift of grandchildren and the gifts He gives to our grandchildren. (You may need an extra sheet of paper for this exercise of gratefulness!)

_____

_____

_____

_____

Petition: (Time: 20-25 minutes)

The man who enters by the gate is the shepherd of his
sheep. The watchmen (grandmothers) open the gate
for him (Jesus) and the sheep (our grandchildren)
listen to His voice. He calls his own sheep,

_____, by name and leads him/her out.
When Jesus has brought out _____, who is His
own, He goes ahead of him/her and His sheep,

_____, follow him because he/she know
His voice. But _____ will never follow a
stranger; in fact he/she will run away from him
because _____ does not recognize a
stranger's voice.   John 10: 2-5

My special and specific requests:

_____

_____

_____

_____

My thoughts and loving declarations:

_____

_____

_____

_____

Final Note:

Just think, one Kingdom day our grandchildren will meet each other and perhaps compare notes! They will have a glorious time talking about how ***their*** grandmother gave herself to praying for them. How clearly they will see the direct correspondence to mercy, grace, protection, blessings – the goodness of God and your prayers. Our partnership on this side of heaven pays sweet rewards and sets up an investment of gold standard no fire will burn away. This is perhaps our finest hour!

Finally, when we cannot physically be close to our grandchildren, our prayers unite our spirits with their spirits. Kind of like the fond term of "soul mates." Something unexplainable and of deep satisfaction happens when we spend time WITH God FOR our grandchildren. Relationships with them, their parents, and especially with our Lord deepens, becomes richer, and so rewarding. Prayer assures us of a way we can enjoy our grandchildren even more as we see them through the Lord's eyes and pray His Word.

So tickled you have chosen to join us. A few of my praying grandmom friends have joined me by sharing an introductory paragraph about their personal experiences. We hope to spark a chain reaction in your spirit that will spur you to continual conversation with God -praying about all things, all the time – until you find you are face to face with your Almighty God & Father, Lord Jesus, and Holy Spirit.

May your time with Him be _extravagant_!

Special thanks to these grandmothers:

Julia Kollmyer

Annette Watson

Meleah Runnells

Jeannie Gibby

Donna Newton

Jan Sutterfield

Tangela Cullum

Kendra Holden

Donna Schroeder

Diane Booth

Carolyn Hardie

Nancy Bingham

Cindy Stockdale

Cindy Rush

Bernadette Post

Kathy Pearson

Debbie Eckert

These women are like family – when you pray together something wonderful happens. We did not realize that our initial swapping of "howdy" as moms would too soon become a swapping of hearts and carry us into our grandmothering years!

I pray each of you who pray with us will experience the same joy!

How I join Paul in thanking God for each one of you mentioning you in my prayers, constantly bearing in mind your work of faith and labor of love and steadfastness of hope in our Lord Jesus Christ. (1Thessalonians 1:2& 3)

Abundant blessings to each of you,

Caryn Southerland

Made in the USA
Charleston, SC
25 September 2014